Property of:......................

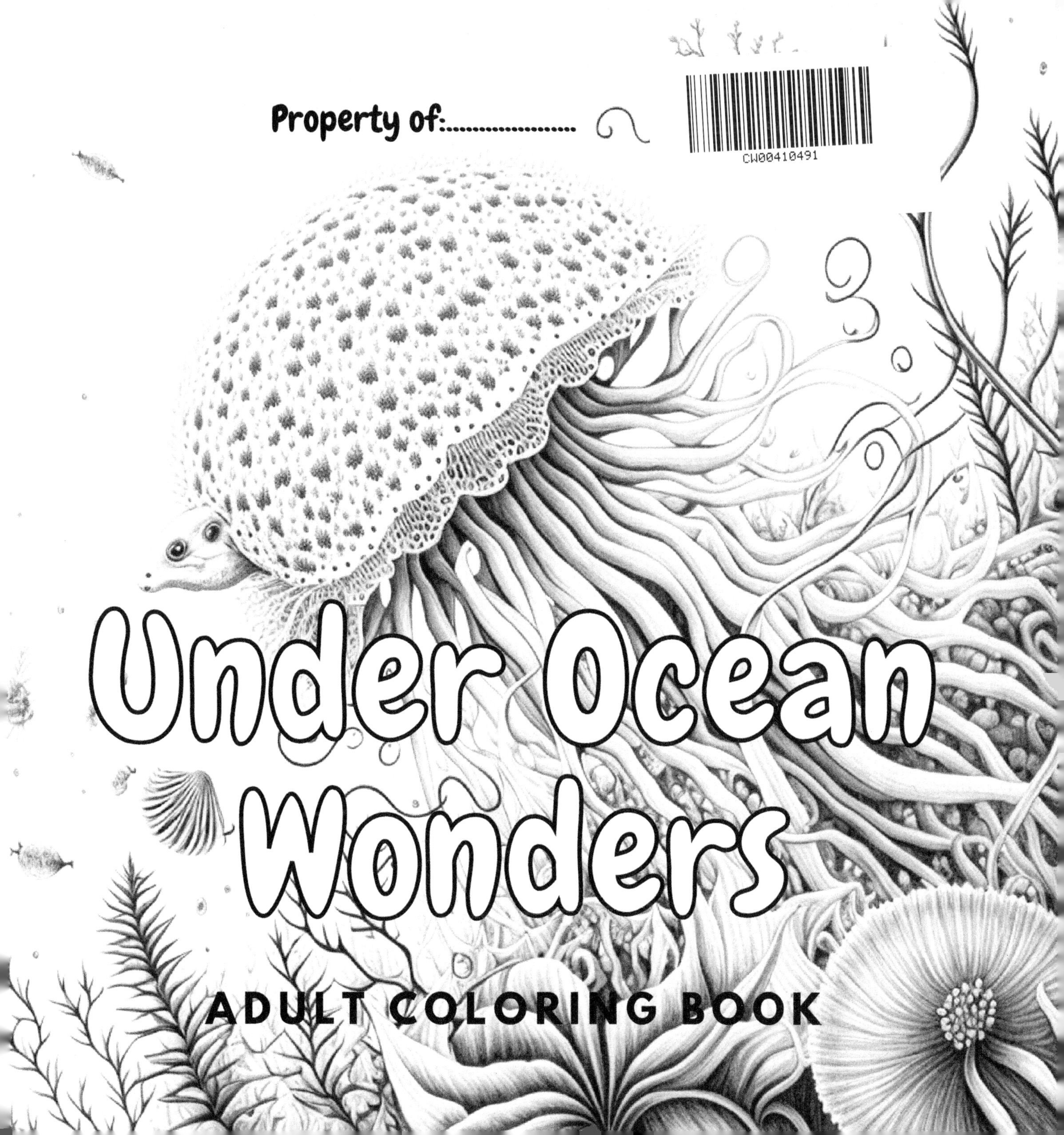

Under Ocean Wonders

ADULT COLORING BOOK

Printed in the USA.

First Edition, January 2023

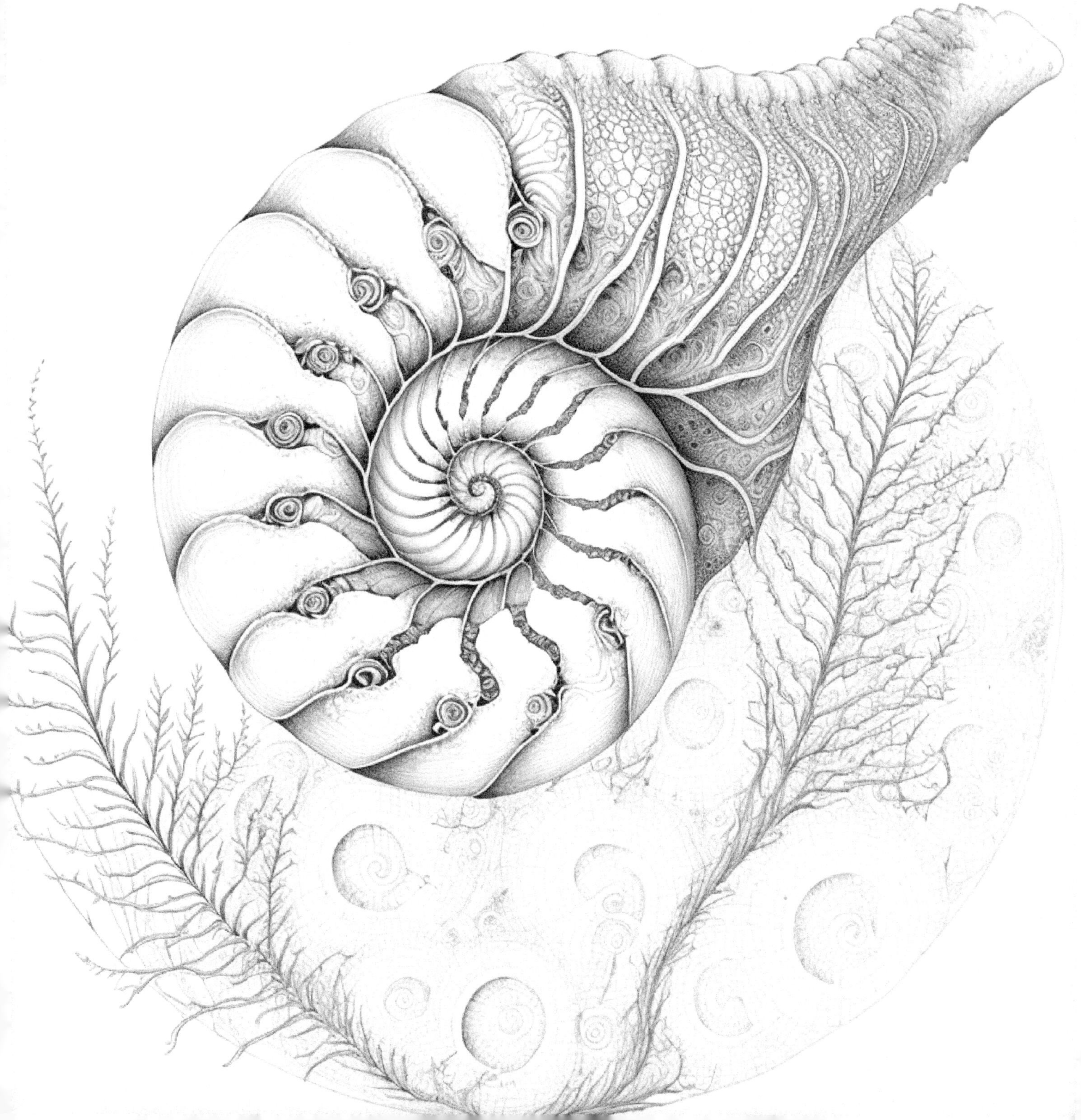

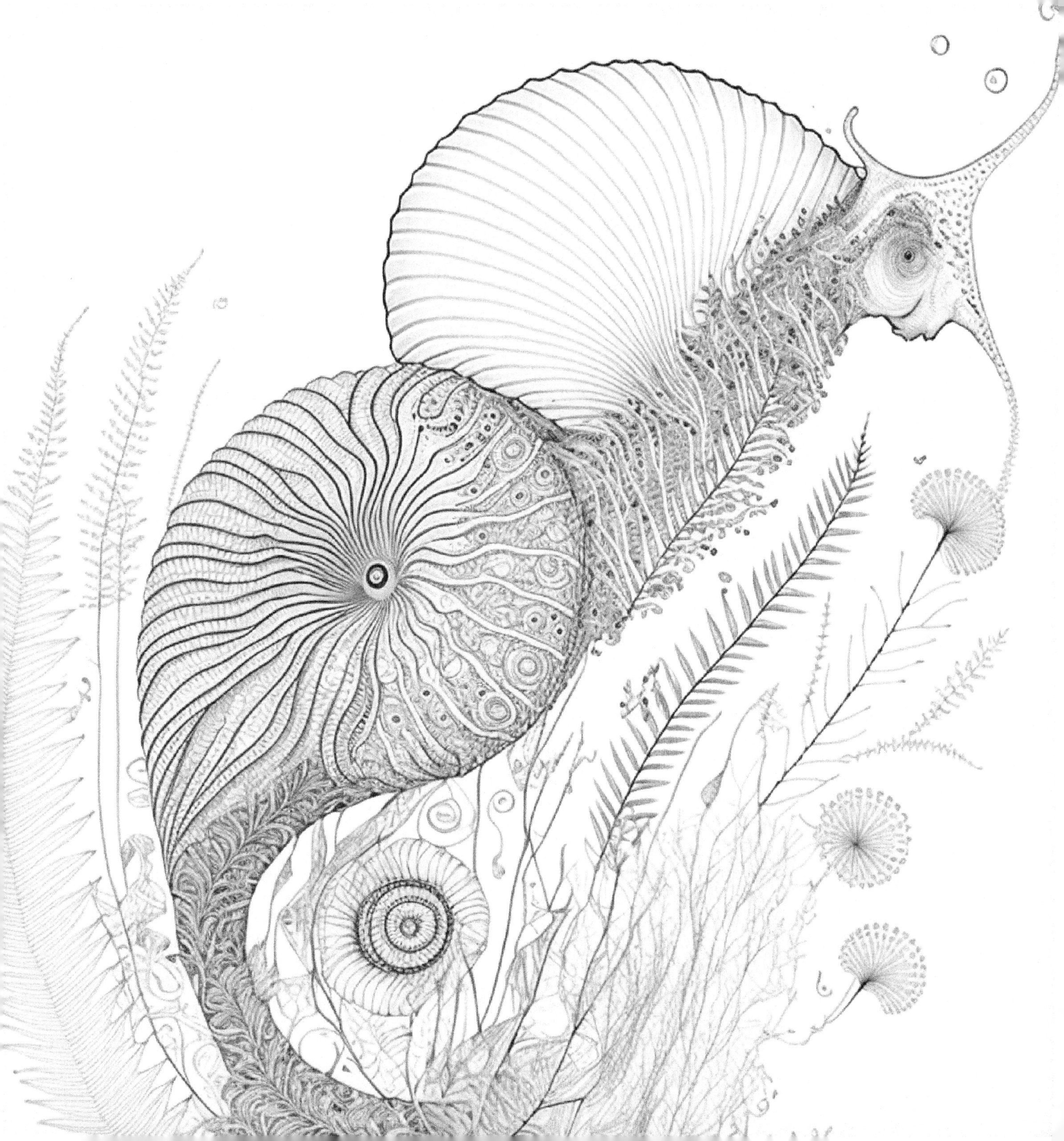

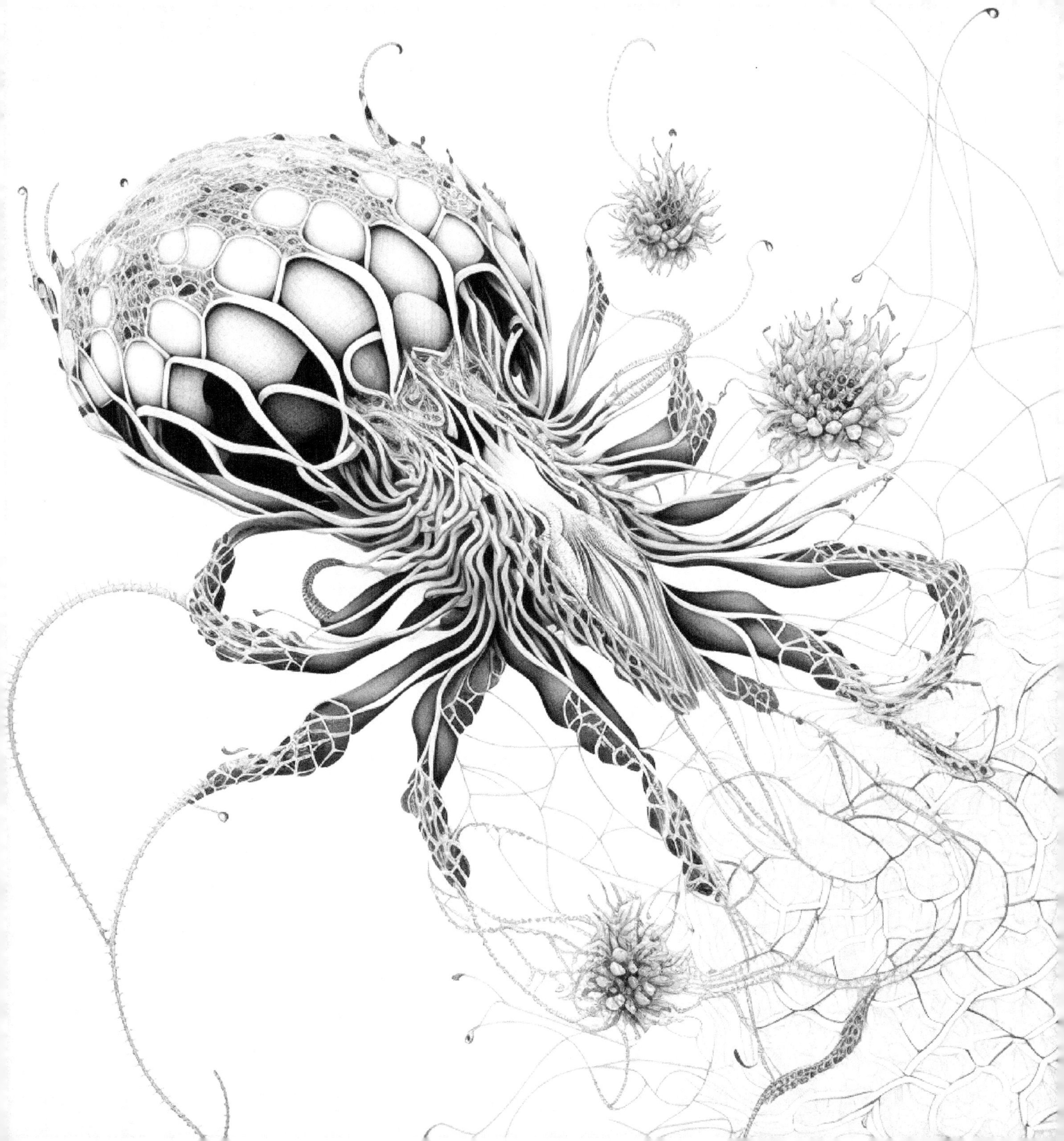

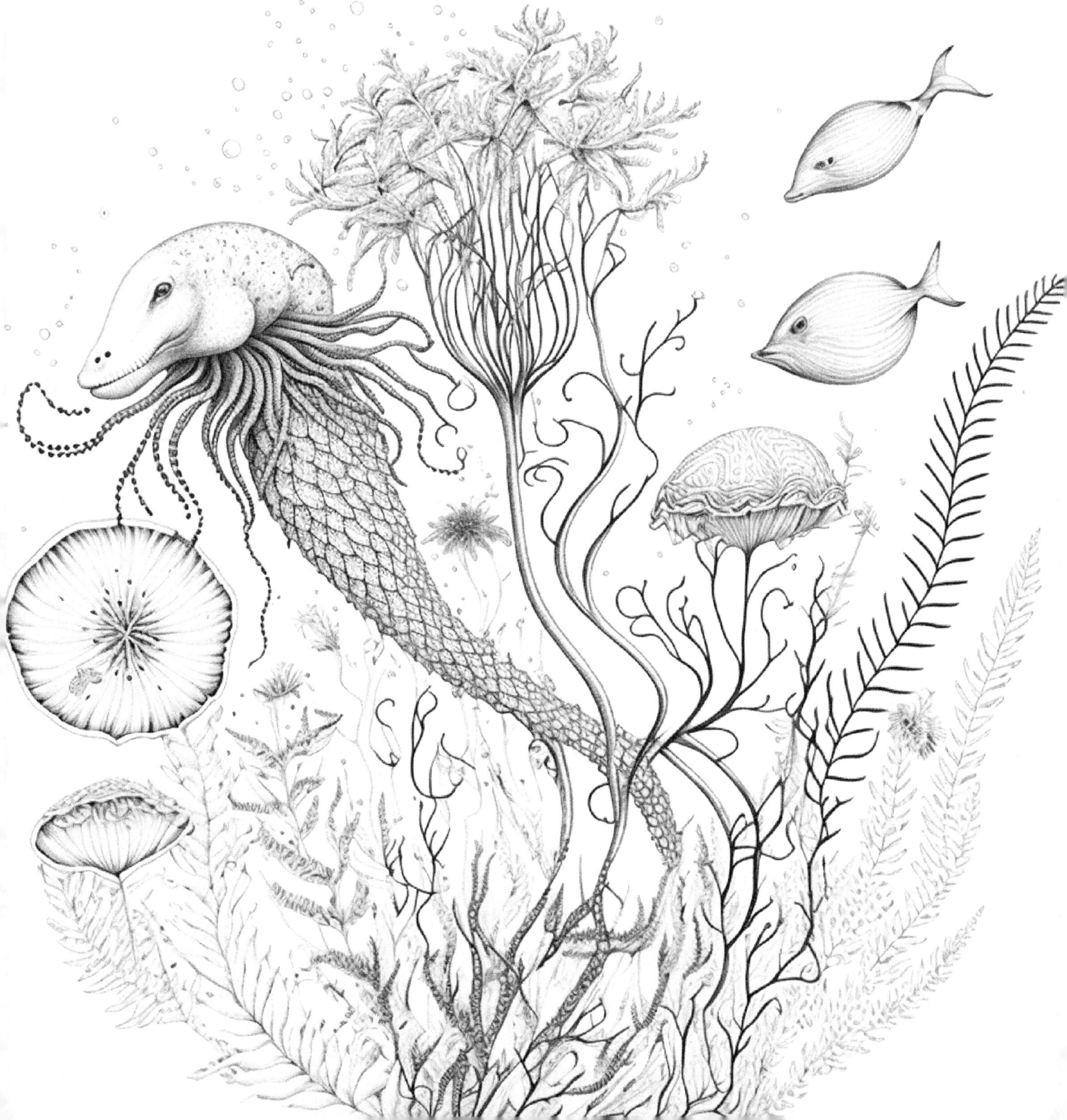

Printed in Great Britain
by Amazon

17343831R00032